1 MONTH OF
FREE
READING

at
www.ForgottenBooks.com

By purchasing this book you are eligible for one month membership to ForgottenBooks.com, giving you unlimited access to our entire collection of over 1,000,000 titles via our web site and mobile apps.

To claim your free month visit:
www.forgottenbooks.com/free831317

ISBN 978-0-483-68673-1
PIBN 10831317

This book is a reproduction of an important historical work. Forgotten Books uses state-of-the-art technology to digitally reconstruct the work, preserving the original format whilst repairing imperfections present in the aged copy. In rare cases, an imperfection in the original, such as a blemish or missing page, may be replicated in our edition. We do, however, repair the vast majority of imperfections successfully; any imperfections that remain are intentionally left to preserve the state of such historical works.

For support please visit www.forgottenbooks.com

ADDRESS

BEFORE THE

HORTICULTURAL SOCIETY

OF

MARYLAND,

BY Z. COLLINS LEE.

JUNE 6, 1839.

ADDRESS

DELIVERED BEFORE THE

HORTICULTURAL SOCIETY

OF

MARYLAND,

AT ITS

ANNUAL EXHIBITION, JUNE 6, 1839,

BY

ZACCHEUS COLLINS LEE, Esq.

BALTIMORE:

JOHN D. TOY, PRINTER.

1839.

BALTIMORE, *June 8th*, 1839.

Z. COLLINS LEE, ESQ.

Dear Sir,—We have been appointed a committee by the Council of the Horticultural Society of Maryland, to obtain from you a copy for publication, of your very beautiful and eloquent oration, delivered before the members of the Society on the evening of the 6th inst.

With many sentiments of regard and esteem, dear slr,

Yours very truly,

T. EDMONDSON, JR.
EDWARD KURTZ.
JOSEPH KING, Jr.
Committee.

———————

BALTIMORE, *June 9th*, 1839.

GENTLEMEN:

I received to-day your very polite letter, requesting a copy of the address delivered by me before the Maryland Horticultural Society on the 6th ult. Having at a short notice attempted, very imperfectly, to perform the pleasing duty assigned to me, in your lovely festival of flowers, 1 now submit the address to you, claiming for it that indulgence which its demerits require, and offerlng it only as a sincere expression of my opinions and best wishes in behalf of your interesting Society.

With sentiments of esteem and friendship, 1 am,

Very respectfully yours,

Z. COLLINS LEE.

To T. EDMONDSON, JR. ESQ.
EDWARD KURTZ, ESQ.
JOSEPH KING, Jr. ESQ.
Committee.

ADDRESS.

LADIES AND GENTLEMEN OF THE

MARYLAND HORTICULTURAL SOCIETY:

AT your request I appear this evening to discharge a pleasing duty, and offer with you on this fragrant and pure shrine of nature, the homage and gratitude, which these her gifts of fruit and flower demand.

From the engrossing and dull pursuits of artificial life—from the marts of commerce and the feverish paths of politics and ambition, we here solicit all ages and classes to unite in a festival and taste a cup unmingled and unembittered by selfishness or pride.

Had I consulted my own just estimate of the occasion and my unfitness to make it interesting or useful, the duty I now perform should have been declined, but there was something so refreshing and beautiful in the associations of your society—that I yielded rather to instinct and feeling than to judgment, and determined to throw myself upon the same kind opinion and indulgence which had called me to its discharge.

2

The anniversaries of national disenthralment and renown are stirring and patriotic in themselves—but the very achievements they celebrate, have been won by the blood of patriots and the sufferings of a whole people—the laurel and the willow entwine the chaplet on the hero's brow ; and many a tear for the gallant dead, saddens the 'flowing bowl' in which their deeds 'are freshly remembered.' In other lands less favoured and free than our own, the waving of banners—the falchion's gleam, and the roar of cannon, proclaim too often the sanguinary triumph of power over civil liberty—and the proud pageant is darkened by the retrospect of battles—the sack of cities—the burning of villages and the flight and massacre of thousands, before the conqueror's sword. Even in the earlier days of chivalry and romance, with the tilt and the tournament where was sung and commemorated,

'Knighthood's dauntless deed,
And beauty's matchless eye'—

there, alas, so servile and degrading a barrier separated the lord from the serf—that it robbed these heroic jubilees of that freshness and attraction which freedom alone bestows.

But this, your anniversary, simple and unostentatious, though it be, is, compared with *those*, the refreshing shower, and the balmy air, after the thunder-cloud has burst, and the summer heat has passed away. It is the *union* of all that is useful with all that is beautiful—the *rainbow* of the fields, displaying every colour and fraught with every sweet.

Surely then, if the smiles of heaven ever descend, it must be upon a scene like this—for you have come up here, the young, the beautiful, the aged, to behold and adore the wisdom and benignity of Him, whose wonderful works are now spread out before us, and to whom human pageants are 'as sounding brass and a tinkling cymbal,' for 'the lilies of the valley are his, and Solomon in all *his* glory was not arrayed like one of these.'

Upon an occasion of such unalloyed interest and pleasure, it would ill become me to detain you with any laboured or scientific dissertation, even had I the ability or the time to do so: I therefore choose rather to dwell on some of the more obvious advantages of your society, and enforce upon the public attention—the claims it so irresistibly presents to more general and zealous support.

The Maryland Horticultural Society was formed in 1832, by a few gentlemen of taste and education, who then determined to give to the long neglected subject their attention; and among its officers and members at that date, will be found several beloved fellow citizens, now no more, associated with many who are still its friends and patrons—they subsequently obtained an act of incorporation which in its preamble declares the object to be an association, 'for the purpose of improving and encouraging

the science and practice of Horticulture, and of in-
troducing into the State, new species and varieties
of trees, fruits, plants, vegetables and flowers.'

The first annual exhibition was held in June, 1833,
and at this, its sixth anniversary, it presents to the
public the most cheering evidences of its beneficial
and successful progress:—To an increased list of
members, it has added and united by its own attrac-
tive pursuits, many of our admired and spirited
townswomen, whose zeal and devotion have already
imparted a charm and impulse to the Society not to
be resisted by the most selfish and obdurate Bene-
dict or misanthrope; while, apart from these attrac-
tions and resources, it is now giving life and energy
to innumerable cultivators of the soil, by awarding
weekly and annual premiums to the most enterprising
and successful among them, and thereby affording to
industry and taste a stimulus, and to Horticulture, a
prominent place among the sister arts—indeed the
present exhibition of flowers alone, might challenge
competition in our country, while the rapid improve-
ments manifested in the culture of fruits and vege-
tables since the Society's foundation, will speak its
best eulogy: and the regret must now arise that, in
this our Baltimore, distinguished for the beauty and
moral loveliness of her daughters, and the valour
and public spirit of her sons, so many years should
have been suffered to elapse in which the culture of
the garden and the husbandry of the field (taught

us thirty years ago by the West Indian emigrant) were without this great auxiliary and stimulant—and that more regard and attention is not now given to the Society.

Around us, and on every hand, our hills and valleys are blooming with the growth of almost every plant and tree, and we are in our walks and rides enchanted by the rich scenes which open from some adjacent and once barren spot, where 'emparadised in flowers,' the cottage of the Horticulturist peeps forth to win the heart and gratify the eye.

Our markets too, in the abundance they offer and the returns they make to the industrious and thrifty farmer and gardener, will convince you, that *interest* as well as pleasure, are moving onward hand in hand in the diffusion and enlargement of the Society's benefits—while by its direct agency, every foot of ground near our city, and landed property generally in its neighbourhood, is rapidly enhanced in value, and by being converted into gardens and rural retreats, afford even to 'the dull edge of sated appetite,' some luscious fruit, or early plant and vegetable, before strangers to our boards—and then, the ornamental trees which embosom so many cool sequestered country seats, where the invalid and man of business may repair for renovation and repose—all proclaim with most 'miraculous organ' the usefulness, and the elegant and refined pleasures of Horticulture.

The great Roman orator declared in one of his finest orations—that there was no better pursuit in life—none more full of enjoyment or more worthy a freeman, than agriculture; the same may be said of the kindred art which gave birth to this Society: and Lord Bacon, the great master of human learning, has borne testimony to its value, in an essay on this subject, in which he describes Gardening and Horticultural avocations, as the purest of human pleasures as well as the greatest refreshments to the spirits of men; and considers the perfection of this art, as the indication of a nation having attained the highest degree of civilization and refinement.—He says in his quaint language 'when ages grow to civility and elegancy; men come to build stately, sooner than to garden finely, as if gardening were the greater perfection.'

The sacred volume also breathes throughout its holy pages, the sanction and encouragement of rural and innocent pursuits; and the Creator by placing our first parents in a garden—a paradise—

> 'And place of rural charms and various views,
> WIth groves whose rich trees wept odorous gum and balm,
> Where flowers of all hues, and without thorn
> The rose untended bloomed'—

seemed indeed to indicate the preference and favour which the husbandman and gardener would ever receive at his hand.

Profane history has brought down to us its mythology and civil rites, associated and invested with fruits and flowers; and the song of the Bacchanal and the lute of Pan, tell of the clustering grape and the overhanging bough. But the knowledge of plants was then greatly limited, and few, very few of the wonderful creations which modern botany has since disclosed, were known or regarded.

The revelations of the Creator to the tenants of Eden, doubtless discovered to them such productions of the earth as were necessary to their sustenance; but the Bible only speaks of the three general divisions of the vegetable world into the *grass*, the *herb*, and the *tree*, and Solomon, the most celebrated for his botanical knowledge, enumerates particularly the Mandrake, the Cedar of Lebanon, and the Hyssop that groweth on the wall, as most prominent in his day.

For centuries afterwards, Botany was but the humble hand-maiden of medicine and surgery; hence we find the balm of Gilead extolled in Judea as the panacea of all diseases, and of more inestimable value than all our modern panaceas for the assuaging of the ills that 'flesh is heir to.'

The heroic age added little or nothing to the preceding period, unless indeed the fabled gardens of the Hesperides and Alcinous, in which Homer has placed 'the reddening apple, the luscious fig, the glowing pomegranate, the juicy pear, the verdant olive, and the bending vine, can be regarded as bright exceptions—these being the offspring rather of poetry than mother earth.

From the days of Theophrastus to those of Pliny, during an interval of nearly four hundred years, there had been only enumerated about six hundred plants, regarded more for their medicinal than nouishing qualities, and the account we have of them is very indistinct and unsatisfactory.—Following came on the darker ages, in which the few known arts of life shared the sad fate of civil liberty, leaving to the world the discovery, by a few Moorish and Arabian physicians, of one or two herbs—such as Rhubarb and Senna, which are now recognized in our materia medica.

The Roman Era, deriving as it did, its taste for gardening from Greece, to the extent it had gone there, opened a wider field to its cultivation. Numerous beautiful passages in the Latin poets prove the high estimation in which gardening was held among the Romans.—Tacitus describes a palace built by Nero, which was on a site laid out on the principles of modern gardening; he says, 'the usual and common luxuries of gold and jewels which adorned this palace were not so much to be admired as the fields, and lakes, and flowers, which here and there opened in prospects before it. But it is to modern times we must look for the revival and creation of botany as a *science*.—Gœsner, Haller, and Linnæus established for it a system of investigation, by which thousands of new and rare pro-

ductions were added to the catalogue of Ceres and
Flora. These great high-priests of nature, reduced
at once, to fixed principles and invariable rules, the
study, and by the classification of plants according
to their natural affinities, demonstrated, that, like
man, their domestic life was regulated and sweeten-
ed by the presence of the gentler sex, and their
being depended upon constitutions and habits pe-
culiar to themselves.

In England, during the reigns of Henry and
Elizabeth, much of the taste and natural beauty of
the gardens of Rome were lost sight of, and substi-
tuted by an artificial and grotesque deformity, which
maintained for many years, and which, by torturing
the box, the yew, and evergreens, into the shape
of beasts and other whimsical forms, degraded the
standard of horticulture—so that many of the Eng-
lish gardens of that period are described, as being
adorned with yew trees in the shape of giants—
Noah's ark cut in holly—St. George and the dragon,
in box—cypress lovers—laureline bears, and all the
race of root-bound monsters which flourished, and
looked tremendous around the edges of every grass
plat.*

But a better spirit soon succeeded, and the works
and philosophy of Dr. William Turner, the father
of English botany and gardening, gave a right direc-

* See the eloquent address of Mr. Poinsett, in 1836, before the Horticul-
tural Society of South Carolina.

tion to its pursuit, and added countless treasures
to the researches of his predecessor—and by the
innumerable varieties of shrubs and flowers, to which
he gave 'a local habitation and a name,' the sea-
girt island became the home and nursery for almost
every tree and plant; and it is now to the annals
of English agriculture and gardening, that we look
for the most valuable improvements in the useful
and ornamental departments of horticulture.

The science of botany, being thus founded solely
on the natural affinities and fixed laws of vegetation,
the great masters to whom I have referred, raised
it at once from being the obscure handmaid of medi-
cine, to be the most enlarged and delightful study to
which the head and heart of man could be devoted.
The poorest plant and the most unobtrusive flower
that 'blushed unseen,'—under their hands in a mo-
ment, unfolded the mysteries of its being, and the
hidden lore of nature. For if the flowers on the
mountains, and in the valleys, are the alphabet of
angels, with which they have written secret and
divine truths upon the hill-tops, how doubly attrac-
tive must become a study, which shall disclose the
loves of those angels, or the higher destiny of man.

Standing as we do, at an immeasurable distance
from the olden time, living in an age and land where
all who have the spirit to be free, or the virtue to be
just, may become public benefactors; how strong
are the calls which duty and interest, in every art

and department of life, make on us, to be active and beneficent in our efforts. If we cast our eyes over the world, its past and present condition, how infinitely exalted appears the physical and intellectual resources of our generation.

The face of nature too, is more prolific and interesting, and exhibits ten thousand beauties and benefits, unknown to past ages.—The history, therefore, of the vegetable world, written as it now is, in every language, and on every green field, developed then but little compared with the present hour, in which we have assembled to celebrate its triumphs, and to behold, by the light of truth and christianity, what was denied to the darker eras of man.

' But the great temple of nature, though thus opened, is not explored, beyond us there are many meandering streams and flowery fields to be traced, and hidden treasures to be discovered.—The promised land rises in bright perspective, and our children must finish what has been commenced by us,— kindling brighter lights, and erecting nobler altars to nature and religion.

· What a theatre for horticultural effort does our own country afford? The vegetation of the United States is as various as its climate and soil.—In the Floridas grow the majestic palm—the orange—the cotton—the indigo, and the sugar-cane. In the Carolinas, the eye of the traveller is charmed with the beauty and grandeur of the forest trees—the ever-green oak—the various species of pine—walnut, and plane tree—the splendid tulip—the curious cypress, and the superb magnolia.

While the oaks, the firs, and the chestnuts of the middle and northern states, afford to the naturalist a rich scene for investigation and study.

Already ten species of the walnut are distinguished for their use and beauty, in the soil and in manufactures, and as many of the maple, the spruce, the hickory, and the larch—most of them now transplanted to our gardens, and public pleasure grounds, are the objects of daily converse and admiration.

There, too, is the giant sycamore, the king of our western forests, exhibiting in its growth, a fit emblem of the vigorous and hardy race, who people the young, but glorious west.—It rises, as Mr. Washington Irving has described it, in the most graceful form, with vast spreading lateral branches, covered with bark of a brilliant white.—These hundred white arms interlacing with the other green forest trees, form one of the most striking traits of American scenery.—A tree of this kind, near Marietta, measured fifteen feet and a half in diameter, and it is said, that Judge Tucker, of Virginia, obtained a section of such a tree—put a roof to it, and furnished it as a study, which contained a stove, bed, and table,—making a comfortable apartment.

Horticulture is domesticating the birch—the elm—the acacia, and the poplar, and beautifying our gardens with the magnolia—the holly—the almond, and the Catawba, and many others, whose existence was almost unknown to us ten years ago.

Some of the most luscious fruits we now prize and cultivate, are strangers to our soil.—Modern horticulture, within the last two centuries, has domesti-cated them.—The fig was brought from Syria, the citron from Medea, the peach from Persia, the pomegranate from Africa, apricots from Epirus, apples, pears, and plums from Armenia, and cherries from Pontus—to Rome they first passed—then to Europe, and with our progenitors, many of them became the pilgrims of freedom in America.

Public gardens of any note and extent, owe also their establishment to modern times.—-The first known in Europe, was that of Lorenzo de Medici, in Florence: afterwards, the celebrated botanic garden of Padua was planted, and flourished in 1533. That of Bologna was also founded by the liberality of Pope Pius the VI. then followed that of Florence, erected by the Grand Duke; since which period they have steadily increased, and there is now one to be found in almost every city of Italy. The botanic garden of Leyden was established in 1577, forty-four years after that of Padua, which it surpassed in number and variety of plants—in 1663, the catalogue of this garden numbered 1,104 species. And in Boerhaave's time, who, when professor of botany there, neglected nothing to augment its riches, it contained 6,000 plants; nearly all the beautiful flowers from the Cape of Good Hope, which now adorn our gardens, were first cultivated there. The first botanic garden in France, was established at Montpelier, in 1597; but the Garden of Plants at Paris was afterwards founded, in 1620, by Louis XIII.—this noble institution has been greatly enlarged by successive monarchs, and is now regarded as the most scientific garden, and the best botanic school in Europe.

A taste for flowers is said to have been introduced into England, by the Flemish emigrants, who fled (as did those of St. Domingo to our state,) to that country, to escape the cruelties of the Duke of Alva, in 1567. The first botanic garden in England was afterwards founded at Oxford; and the royal gardens at Kew, were begun about the middle of the eighteenth century, by Frederick, Prince of Wales, father of George the Third, and now contain a rich and extensive collection of exotics, equalled, however, if not surpassed by those in the botanic garden at Liverpool; an institution founded by the influence and efforts of Mr. Roscoe, who established it in 1800.

In our country we know of no extensive establishment of this description—that commenced by Dr. David Hosack, of New York, has been suffered to go to decay by the government of the State, who purchased it from the learned and enterprising proprietor.—Here, in Maryland, there is as yet no public garden of the kind—but our Society is we trust awakening public attention to the subject.

A taste is now springing up amongst us—and many private gardens beautifully represented here to-night, attest the success of individual efforts. The field is before us—labourers are wanted—its limits are the confines of our republic.—Look to the south, clothed at this time in a garb of rural splendour, to which its tropical flowers and brilliant evergreens, give a surpassing lustre.—There alone flourishes the live oak, that tree, which upon the ocean is the bulwark of our land and the boast of our prowess. How irresistible and magical is the march of improvement, and the triumph of culture and art? Let the rover or naturalist seek some cool sequestered spot by the sources of the Missouri or the Mississippi, and pleased with the bright and lively rill which dances from rock to rock, to the murmuring cadence of its own music, watch and follow it as it steals under the osier and the vine with gentle wing till he finds it; the majestic river upon whose bank wealth builds his palace—science his temple, and religion her sacred fane; could his wonder be greater or his joy more intense than ours at the triumphs of art and refinement over the rudeness of uncultured nature? Methinks the progenitors of many who hear me, once sought the fresh breeze of the evening, and plucked the scented wild flower on *this very spot,* now covered and adorned by edifices of taste and splendour, and crowded with monuments of civilization.—So rapid and imperceptible therefore are the improvements of the great age, that if we would preserve around us at all the pristine charms of hill and dale, of wild flowers and native forests, it must be by horticulture and in our gardens.—For the hammer and the noise of the busy multitude, and the axe of the emigrant, and the sweep of commerce, and the sister arts, are onward with the velocity of our rail roads, clearing the way and settling the waste places, for more enduring power, and extended wealth than the woods and wilds of our native soil can afford.

Our national resources, too, physical and political; and the giant strides of our people, already proclaim, even beyond the Mississippi, the sway of civil institutions, and the glories of freedom: hurried before their resistless march, the red man and his once countless tribes, is flying from his hunting grounds and council fires—and his lion heart and eagle eye has cowered before the victorious arm of the white man.

Scarce two hundred years have rolled away, since the rock of Plymouth, and the heights of Jamestown were pressed by pilgrims' feet, and consecrated to human rights.—Now twenty-six commonwealths, bounded by the Atlantic and the Gulf of Mexico, are before us, united by a common bond, and flourishing under the same bright banner, and crowded with upwards of fifteen millions of freemen.—What a spectacle for the world to admire! what a cause of self-gratulation to us?

The 'May Flower,' laden with the seeds of liberty, touched *then* with drooping sails a savage and inhospitable shore—*now*, from the same strand, the moving palaces of steam and the countless ships of commerce, depart and arrive between cities of astonishing wealth and population. I repeat it that now is the time for our most active exertions in the noble cause of Agriculture, and its patron, Horticulture—if we desire to keep pace with the wide spreading manufactures and commerce of our union.

To the farmer and agriculturist is offered a climate and soil more fertile, varied and healthy than any under the sun, combining the heat of the tropics with the temperatures of the north and west, and inviting him to cultivate every variety of produce: while the growth of distinct and inexhaustible staples, presents what is no where to be found under the same government, agricultural resources of priceless value, which can in no event compete with and oppose each other, in the same foreign or domestic market.

The south; opulent in the mimic snow of the cotton and the golden harvests of the rice field, binds the planter to his soil by the strong tie of *interest*, and makes his staple the very life's blood of exchange and commerce; while the northern, western

4

and middle States, by their grain and the culture of tobacco, form a vast store-house and granary for domestic aud exporting uses, unlike the granaries of Rome, inexhaustible, and not filled from plundered provinces.

I might dilate upon these animating motives to exertion, which our favoured position and resources so strongly urge—but I forbear, pausing only to add, that if the cause of agriculture and the claims of this society have no recommendation from considerations like these, there is yet *one precious and irresistible motive*, to be found in the opinions and practice of him, the mention of whose name raises a throb of gratitude in every heart that loves liberty.—Among the letters preserved and published of the immortal Washington, is one addressed by him in 1782, to Mr. Young, an English horticulturist, in which the Father of his country, uses the following language :

'Agriculture in the field and garden has ever been among the most favourite of my amusements, though I never have possessed much skill in the art, and nine years, total inattention to it, has added nothing to a knowledge which is best understood from practice.' He then desires his correspondent to send him the following horticultural items :

'A little of the best kind of cabbage seed for the field culture—twenty pounds of the best turnip seed—ten bushels of sanfoin seed—eight bushels of winter vetches—two bushels of rye grass seed, and fifty pounds of best clover seed.' What a touching illustration of the simple habits and practical sense of this illustrious man.—At the time this letter was penned, he had just returned victorious from the revolutionary struggle to the shades of Mount Vernon ;—we there find him turning from the voice of praise and the blaze of military glory to his *farm* and *garden*—with the same fondness with which the infant seeks the maternal bosom, and in the unostentatious amusements and healthful exercises of his fields, becoming the first American farmer, as he had proved himself the greatest hero and general on the tented plain.

What a lesson and rebuke should this incident convey to the noisy pride and bustling littleness of some of the miscalled great men of our day.—To the *placeman* and demagogue, even the garden of Mount Vernon, blooming under the eye and hand of Washington, could afford no charm or solace for the loss of power or emolument—*these* serve their country but to *serve themselves.*—Marius in his defeated hour, sighed amid the ruins of Carthage, and the imperial exile wept upon a barren rock.—Washington, whether at the head of armies or guiding the destinies of his country, was the same exalted character ; simple in his tastes, manly and noble in all the relations of life.—In him education found a patron, religion and virtue a model and support, and agriculture its most distinguished benefactor.—So happily combined were his sentiments, taste and principles, that in private as in public life, his example will descend to unnumbered generations, as the brighest ever bequeathed by man to man.

Imagination might carry those of us who have visited the hero's tomb, to that sequestered and beautiful garden with its nursery of rare exotics and tropical fruits—the classic arrangements of its boxwood and hawthorn hedge, and the simple but chaste display of every flower and plant which wealth or fancy could procure.—-There upon *this* seat sat Washington when the storm and battle was over, and refreshed his spirit and elevated his thoughts by the culture and contemplation of his garden—beside him was her, the chosen and beloved consort and companion of his life—like him in the noble but gentler attributes of her mind, fitted to be the sharer of his glory and repose.—Around them bloomed the gifts of every clime, from the rose and fragrant coffee shrub of Java to the night budding Cereus of Mexico.

The seat still remains, but the patriot sleeps at the foot of that garden by the side of his fond associate and exalted partner,—wild flowers and the evergreen are blooming over them, in token of the renewal and immortality of the glorious dead.—And when summer comes—there the birds sing sweetly, and like angels' voices, do they tell of happiness, harmony and peace.

The sculptured column, and proud mausoleum might (and should) adorn that spot—but in the scene as nature's hand has left it—in the murmurs of the breeze, the majestic flow of the Potomac, and the solemn stillness of the grove, broken only by the wild bird's note—above all, in the yet unfaded and unaltered walks of that *garden* of *Washington* there is a *memorial*, which the 'storied urn or animated bust could never give.' It is the *pathos* and *truth* of *nature*.—This theme is carrying me beyond my purpose—you will pardon the digression—I must pause.

Before us this evening is spread out a rich banquet—the strawberry and cherry,—the more substantial offerings for the kitchen are here, also, presenting a rotundity and condition which an alderman might envy ; among them there doubtless is, that talisman of fortune—the golden fleece of the vegetable world—I allude to the morus multicaulis, for the culture of which, it is feared, all things else may be abandoned ; so warm is the fever which its prosperous fortunes have excited, that, it is said, 'a loving swain in one of the fertile counties on the Eastern Shore, was breathing to his lady-love the most empassioned vows, and had put the solemn and interesting question, upon a favourable answer to which his happiness depended, when she, with much enthusiasm, replied by asking him another question, do you grow the *morus multicaulis?* Oh! no, he exclaimed, *only* beautiful flowers and roses for *you.*' Alas! simple youth, this answer was fatal to his hopes, and the *morus multicaulis* prevailed over *love.* Horticulture, in addition to this, is colonizing trees and shrubs, for the purposes of shade and ornament for the bowers of love.—Should it not then command the affections and aid of the fair?

There are finally to be drawn from the reflections of this anniversary, many lessons and benefits, calculated to warm the heart with gratitude to Him, who is the giver of all things; and above all, there are opened, by the study of this volume of nature, sources of unfailing joy and contentment. So ordered is the economy and wisdom of heaven, that this lovely season of the year,—the precursor of Ceres, and the prophet of abundant harvest, by its *regular return* teaches 'desultory man, studious as he is, of change,' that here is an invariable and immutable law, stamped upon every plant that grows, and every bud that opens, alike incapable of change and deterioration, and instructs the child of adversity, who has been left alone, scathed like the pine upon the mountain's top, by the lightning and the tempest, that there is a recuperative principle in the mind, shadowed forth most beautifully by the reviving tree and the budding flower, which the breath of heaven shall awaken to *life, beauty,* and *immortality.*—Emblems of the christian's hope, which burns brighter as the clouds gather, and his spirit is departing, and his heart becoming cold.

By assiduous efforts and gentle care do we not, when this lovely season is gone, behold how culture and the artificial warmth of the conservatory and the green-house keep a perennial spring about us amid the snows of winter, and the window and boudoir of woman become the home of the dahlia and the rose, living and giving out their incense to her tender mercies, when all around is death; or blooming in unwonted splendour among her soft tresses, telling of the kind, gay girl, the fond and loving mother, whose hand has watered them, and beneath whose smile their buds have expanded into life.

The sentiment and morality of flowers are among the most attractive of their charms; who does not feel full often the pure power of the teachings which these little moralists declare. The rose is a legend of romance, and its history, whether in the bower of love, or embroidered on the banners of civil war, is a history of the *heart*.—The rose of Sharon, and the lilies of Damascus, were sung by the waters of Israel, while poetry and religion have associated and embalmed it with all the most sacred of their rights.

In the festive hall, where the dance, and song, and music prevail, *it* is the companion and emblem of the young and joyous.—The bridal wreath and the nuptial altar find in *its* purity and fragrance, though but 'the perfume and suppliance of an hour,' a sentiment congenial with the brightness and brevity of the passing scene.

And, oh, with what unsearchable and deep love does the youthful mother place *it* in the garland of her first born; and should the nursling be *too* early snatched from her bosom, with what fond but melancholy pleasure will she oft times turn with moistened eye from the memory of the cherished one, to the rose bud or the flower, as the remembrancer of its loveliness and beauty. Think you there is then no truth in all this? To the pensive and uncorrupted mind can there be a pleasure more refined than the culture of these sweet earth-born innocents, amid the shades and serenity of the garden and the groves?

The Prince de Ligné, who was the companion of monarchs, and surrounded by the splendour of courts, derived his chief enjoyment from the cultivation of his graden, and with enthusiasm has said, 'would that I could warm the whole world with my taste for gardening; it appears to me impossible that a *bad man* can possess it; there is no virtue that I do not imagine in him who loves to speak of, and to make gardens; fathers of families, inspire your children with a love of gardening and flowers.' This is the language of a prince, and the testimony of a generous and exalted spirit.

There is, besides, in the culture of the garden, a *religion* silently but truly taught, to which meditation gives the most consoling tone; the conflict of exclusive and *intolerant* opinions are there unfelt and unheard, but we hold converse with nature, and from her flowery lap raise our eyes and hearts in adoration to Him, who,

> 'Not content with every food of life
> To nourish man; by kind illusions
> Of the wondering sense, hath made all nature
> *Beauty* to his eye and *music* to his ear.'

How cooling to the chafed brow and the care-worn spirit is the copse-wood shade and the rural walk? What memories of happy days and well-beloved companions crowd upon the garden's contemplative hour, bringing back to age its golden morn, its blithesome boyhood: if a father or a mother hath departed from us, the haunts they loved, the flowers they nursed, the paths they trod, summon us back to all we owe them, and all we have lost in them:

> 'Soft as the memory of buried love,
> Pure as the prayer that childhood wafts above,'

come back to us from these interviews with nature, our best days and our most cherished affections.

The stars have been called the poetry of heaven, but may we not with equal truth turn to these flowers as the poetry of earth, speaking as they do to us of peace and good will among men.

Rank, power, and wealth, the arm of the warrior, and the tongue of the sage, have seldom blessed their possessors; and we are called too often to de-

plore in this and other lands, the evils which have
resulted from the 'fears of the brave and the follies
of the wise.'

How touchingly beautiful and sublime are the
pictures of those primitive days, when under their
own vines and fig trees, the babbling brook at their
feet, and the bleating and spotless flock around them,
the shepherds of Israel poured forth their morning
song of praise to Him who made the meadows to
nourish, and the trees to shade them, with what
fervour did they exclaim, 'The Lord is our shep-
herd we shall not want, he maketh us to lie down
in green pastures and leadeth us beside the still
waters.' The altars of christianity never burned
with a purer incense than this: and are we not then
invoked now to realize from the pursuits of this
Society the primitive charms and excellence which
they impart?

Peace and abundance cover our land—in others
less happy and exalted, some flower or shrub is
the household and tutelary emblem and watch-
word of national honour. The lily of France and
the rose of Burgundy, have encountered the thistle
and the shamrock on the bloody field, or interwoven
in peace become the olive branch and pledge of
union and friendship—with us as yet, not one of
the many beautiful productions of our soil is the
badge of American freedom.—And why should it
not be, like the song which animates in the fight—

let us also point to some ever present and blooming token of our land, which will meet us in the field, cheer us in absence, and delight us every where, and which to the dying patriot's eye shall revive the recollection of his home and country—

'Sternitur infelix alieno vulnere ; cœlumque
Aspicit, et dulces moriens reminiscitur Argos.'

To fix then upon this emblem is a task I commend to our fair countrywomen, who should indeed, present it as a gift from the beautiful to the brave, with which to return victorious, or return no more.

These are the refined charms of Horticulture, and thus is your Society recommended :—At this celebration it invites men of all conditions in life to come forward here, in Maryland, and devote not their gold and silver, but their leisure and taste to the most interesting cause and the most delightful recreation.—The motives, the land we inhabit, the resources of our people, and the innate value and purity of the pursuit itself, have been alluded to, and all call on us to lend our influence to its promotion.—The tired and worn down citizen shall be refreshed by it, for to green fields and healthful exercises we introduce him while living ; and there is a spot preparing for him, when dead, almost within sight of this hall, a place of repose,—a city of silence, which by the enterprise of many connected with this Society, shall ere long realize the prophet's vision that made paradise the home of the dead.

Beneath the fragrant birch and the refreshing evergreen shall *there* repose the departed, with birds to sing over their graves, and the sweetest wild flowers to bloom in earnest of the spirit's destiny.— Horticulture is doing this, then by all its pleasures, by its usefulness and innocency, we do again invoke you to become its patrons and friends.

The studies of the closet and the feverish pursuits of life, wear down the body and corrode the spirit; but here is a pursuit full of beauty and freshness, peaceful and lovely are its ways, pure and uncontaminated is the cup of its joys; its study and culture will assuage anger, moderate ambition and sanctify love, and raising the heart from objects of temporary interest, place it on those of eternal hope—keep with us and about us the bloom and fragrance of life's weary journey, and make us wiser and better in our day and generation.